AF730761

CLIMBING KILIMANJARO SAVED MY LIFE

A Picturesque Journey Triumphing over Evil, One Mountain at a Time

By Author and Photographer XX

I have chosen XX as my pen name
to represent myself as one of the many little girls
who have fiercely survived trauma,
but have felt its brutality.

Specific details of the traumas I have survived are not revealed,
but my triumph over their evil is,
up one beautiful mountain at a time.

I hope my short story depicted here inspires others
to seek victory over the dregs of trauma's anguish,
one monumental step at a time…

The devastation of being robbed of innocence had been one thing, but having been betrayed by the only support I had as a little girl had caught up with me, and I was drowning…until I climbed Kilimanjaro. I ran, yes ran, to the summit even after hiking 10 hours from 14,000 to 19,341ft.

I got so giggly at 18,500 ft. Laughing and stumbling and laughing again. But, when I hit 19,000 ft I had so much energy and clarity. I had never felt so alive! My head had never been clearer. I was consciously inhaling deeply to gather any oxygen molecules in my vicinity. I was breathing so intently, and I was calm. I felt so free, but I didn't know why…

Throughout my journey up Kilimanjaro, conscientious breathing seemed to have uncluttered my mind of the fear of potentially failing to summit. I was excited and at ease at the same time. Breathing deeply, conscientiously, I swam in satisfaction with every move of my upward journey. I was in control of my destiny as much as Mother Nature's weather and land integrity would allow. Even if I chose to not complete the climb, I was in control. I was in love with every moment, and with each cherished step, I oversaw my destiny, trusting that I would succeed at choosing to continue to climb, or succeed at deciding not to, should Mother Nature call me off the mountain. But, with Mother Nature's permission, I carried onward and upward, believing in myself that I had prepared properly to summit…and I enjoyed every single moment of it.

Climbing Kilimanjaro truly saved my life. My glee of having summited did not save me; my control over my destiny did. At 19000+ ft I could breathe like never before. Within a moment of sensing clarity at the top, my mind changed, my life changed…

I FINALLY WANTED TO BE ALIVE.

After descending Kilimanjaro, a phone call from my past immediately reminded me of intensely grotesque trauma and evil betrayal. That post-trekking phone call metaphorically scratched the record needle out of a beautiful track in my mind and replaced it with utterly despicable chatter. My mind moved from a state of bliss to that of disbelief that I *still* had to fight such a war. The soundtrack of a repeated horror movie had momentarily seized control of my turntables…but not for long. Suddenly, my clarity at the summit started making sense: Subconsciously I had set out to conquer what had happened to me as a child, to take control of my body and my mind, and to show myself I am safe in my own hands. I knew I needed more mountain time, preparing for climbs and treks, setting out calculating and controlling my own *choice of "stress,"* and either achieving my goal to climb on or *choosing* to return empty of a summit push. My own, self-guided negotiations on mountainous adventures were my ammunition to squash my mental anguish of past trauma.

Years later, climbing at sea level, I was not thinking about breathing. After all I was at sea level with plentiful oxygen. But, a brilliant mountaineer suggested that I conscientiously breathe before starting a climb and remember to breathe with every move. With each intentional breath, I immersed deeper into the moment. I enjoyed every hold, every bodily position needed to advance up the steep face. I felt like a ballerina floating and dancing up the mountain. I soaked in Mother Nature's creativity that had chiseled every hand hold and foot hold leading to her majestic peak. Breathing intently found me a flow state for the very first time.

Breathing, though, could be done on beaches, on rocky coasts, on paved roads, and in mountains alike. Breathing's calming effect to quell stress could be found anywhere. What made conscientious breathing in the mountains so transformative? So special?

Merging the power of conscientious breathing with the power of preparing for and executing an alpine ice climbing adventure in Central Asia answered my question. Through research, I grasped the concept of the power of choosing to set out on a mission in the mountains, especially at altitude, with its planning and eventual execution. Summiting did not even have to enter the equation. Power stemmed from my setting forth and returning in control of my destiny. Weather conditions permitting a summit push was considered a bonus. Preparing to summit was one lesson. Journeying to a peak or turning around confident in a decision that summiting was not in the cards was lesson two. Identifying control of my destiny, though, was the ultimate prize.

Mountaineering at higher altitudes seemed to push mental chatter reminding me of childhood trauma out of my mind. My mind had to work quickly with limited oxygen, when the blink of an eye was all the time I had to make the choices needed to maintain my course. There was no time for conversations or to "look up the answers," so there was certainly no time to spare on rumination. The repeated calculation of careful steps, the solving of projected climbs, and the mental focus to negotiate ice with massive spikes all seemed to declutter my mind from dwellings on past trauma.

PS. Swinging ice axes into sheets of ice is quite the "stress release," all the while being a means to reach new heights, literally and figuratively! 😉

By actively choosing to place myself in the mountains, I had taken control of my fate. I had the ability to prepare for the mission, and to choose its day, land and weather conditions permitting. And, on the appointed day I had the choice to climb or not to climb. Using my instincts and survival skills I had taken control of my choices in the mountains. By breathing to calm my nervous system in acutely "stressful" situations I learned that "problems"—as routes are called in the climbing world—did not necessarily equate to catastrophic stresses. The problems were solvable. And, I had the power to solve them. That ultimate control over my destiny in a series of chosen "stresses" triggered my understanding of why adventuring up a massive mountain changed my life forever, for the better.

The genius advice of a mountain guide reminding me to breathe when climbing has transcended not only into other sporting realms, but into life's challenges way beyond anything I could have imagined. Repeatedly breathing through "problem-solving" in the mountains, I have been better able to breathe through life's "problems." Those breaths have calmed my stress response, especially with triggers of trauma memories, and have brought calmness to fight-or-flight situations. Having the power to breathe my way to calmness has brought me control over my body and mind. I have begun to feel safe in my own skin as sole protector of my survival. More control over my responses to my environment has lowered my baseline stress to a quieter level. Stresses have become less intense as my baseline stress level has started to sink. Life's problems are weighted, and my responses equate to their intensity, but a baseline of calmness and confidence in bodily and mind autonomy have given me the upper hand in fighting storms head on, with one conscientious, mind-clearing breath at a time.

For me, the mountains have provided brief, repetitive, fight-or-flight modes with consequential instinctual reactions, teaching me a repeated lesson that newly emerging stresses can quickly be resolved. Learning that stress can be instinctually resolved has calmed nervous spikes more and more quickly with greater and greater ease. Essentially, I have been better taming an inner beast. Lack of stress isn't what has made me satisfied, it has been the overcoming of that stress. And, repeatedly calming stress has given me the power to keep pushing through to seek new goals despite setbacks, traumas, or roadblocks, if you will, in the mountains…and elsewhere.

With more hikes, treks, and climbs my mind's turntables have started to play more bliss and less horror. I have been able to take charge, one distant journey at a time. With each mountainous adventure I have continually been waking up from a mind warped by trauma and betrayal. I have found trust in someone to feel safe, and that someone was and is I. It has taken quite a few journeys to fully understand and feel this reality. It has been quite a ride, but I have seen absolutely amazing places because of it.

Having chosen to mostly voyage alone, many people have asked if I am scared to do so in places so far from familiarity. Scared? No. My worst traumas have happened at "home" and my most familiar circles have betrayed me. As a child I wished that I had never been born, and familiar places felt like a trap. Since coming of age to adventure alone, the unknown world has not been a scare. It has been an escape.

Adventuring alone has provided me chances to restore my soul one encounter at a time. It has handed me the reins to control my destiny. It has given me the control over preparations, the ability to correct or learn from oversight or from mistakes, the ability to decide to summit or choose to turn back mid-route, to climb up waterfalls or icefalls or to plunge into crystal mountain pools. Venturing solo, I have been in control of catching my own breaths taken away only by eye-wateringly beautiful views. With each calculated step and conscientious breath, I have proclaimed myself as my protector, and have become free, on one unbeaten path at time.

Venturing alone has provided me with self-reassurance that I can fully take care of myself, that independently I am safe. To me adventuring alone is not bravery; it is survival.

Although voyaging solo has been my favorite way to adventure, some mountains have required a guide, so I sought guides that would take on a solo traveler. The mountains requiring a guide have been more challenging, more demanding of time and energy not just to climb, but to prepare for physically, mentally, and logistically. To all of my guides, you have not only led me up mountains, you have also helped me to move them. On your guided routes, with each swing of an ice axe, step up a steep slope, and pull on a crimp, mountainous problem-solving has built my abilities to squash life's stresses before they could squash me. With each progression, my conscientious breaths have drawn me into the moment and out of the darkness, truly making me feel more and more alive as if wanting to breathe over and over again for the first time. For me, those cherished breaths have been paramount in triumphing over evil. Your mountain guiding has led me to a life of proverbial light only control over my destiny could procure. I have truly wanted to live, with control over my destiny, and with confidence that the stress of traumas will continue to disappear. On many journeys I had not realized why I felt so refreshed at the time, but I have grown to appreciate the opportunities your expertise has afforded my soul. ☺️

Mother Nature has always had the upper hand, but nothing else has stood in my way to climb…but myself. Repeatedly overcoming sought after and calculated "stresses" has transcended many aspects of my life, teaching the lesson that stress doesn't have to mean danger, and taking the reins of control over situations can create a sense of self-safety. Repeated mountain journeys have cycled me through challenges that have ultimately afforded me mental strength. Just as my cardiovascular endurance and striated muscle strength have grown through breakdown and repair, my mind has benefited from controlled stresses triggering repair to build back stronger in preparation for a "next time."

My epiphany that I could triumph over trauma emerged from seeking a mountain route, preparing for it, and making whatever of it Mother Nature allowed for up Kilimanjaro. Adventuring up mountains continues to better shape my mind, reassure me that I can navigate the rise over life's obstacles, and continue to script victory over darkness. Yes, things could go wrong on such escapades, but losing physical life on an adventure would not be dying. It would be living in control of my best life, freely and victoriously over darkness, and triumphing in the warmest of light…

To the Mountains around the World:

Thank you for staging
my triumph over darkness
from The Artic to The Tropics,
from Iceland to Namibia,
from Oman to Mauritius,
from Tibet to Thailand,
from East Asia to West,
and especially from Tasmania to Tanzania.

Your powerful energy
has run deep through my soul.

Thank you for being the foundation of my renaissance...

Made in United States
Troutdale, OR
11/03/2026

56844450R00019